Chapters

This is a work of fiction. Names, characters, places and incidents either are products of the author's imagination or are used fictitiously.

An Unhappy Beginning

Some lives seem destined for trouble from the very start. So it was for Nicholas Perry, whose path was set the moment he was born under uncertain circumstances in Ukraine in 1992. Given up for adoption as an infant, Nicholas was taken in by a couple in Pennsylvania eager to raise a child of their own.

Though his adoptive parents provided a comfortable upbringing, Nicholas struggled emotionally from a young age. The nagging question of why his birth parents abandoned him cast a shadow over his childhood, leaving him with deep feelings of worthlessness. Diagnosed with depression and behavioral disorders early on, Nicholas acted out frequently, desperately seeking attention and validation.

Through it all, he found solace in music, discovering an uncanny talent for the violin. Playing transported Nicholas to a different realm, bringing structure and meaning to his turbulent inner world. For the first time, he felt recognized and praised for something he excelled at. The violin became Nicholas' lifeline, his purpose amid the chaos.

As a teenager, Nicholas came out as gay, embracing his identity with his family's full support. But he continued to feel like an outsider, spending long hours alone composing and practicing. Though passionate and gifted, Nicholas struggled to form meaningful connections – a void that would have dire consequences later in life.

Upon finishing school, Nicholas set out for New York City to pursue his musical dreams. But the cutthroat environment quickly disillusioned him. Without the emotional resilience required to withstand professional disappointments, Nicholas floundered.

It was in the depths of this crisis that he turned to food for comfort. At first an innocent indulgence, his penchant for binge eating morphed into a dangerous obsession – one that would soon consume him whole.

Little did Nicholas know, as he stepped off the train with stars in his eyes, he was entering a city that would nearly destroy him. The constant gaze of millions would impart the validation he craved, but at a devastating cost. His desire for connection would be warped and preyed upon, reducing him to a mere object of consumption.

For in today's world of extremes, even a simmering void within can be twisted into perverse fulfillment with the help of prying eyes. And those void-filled souls who crave attention most are often willing to sacrifice everything for their moment in the glare.

So the stage was set for Nicholas' sordid tale. A fragile psyche, an impenetrable city, and the hungry maw of faceless masses poised to enable his downfall. The elements were in place for a spectacular unravelling – a riveting cautionary tale of fame and isolation; disorder and dependence. Nicholas' story is one of stardom and self-destruction, a Shakespearean tragedy for the digital age. For in the absence of meaning, even darkness can become blinded by the light.

A Fatal Attraction

Nicholas then moved to Colombia. Nicholas' initial days in Colombia with his boyfriend Orin were blissful. Gone were the harsh realities of New York and the disappointment of his floundering music career. In Orin's modest apartment, Nicholas finally felt free to just be himself, happy and in love.

The pair passed countless evenings engrossed in conversation, bonding over their shared passion for health and spirituality. Orin was the first person who truly appreciated Nicholas' immense sensitivity and artistic nature. For his part, Nicholas admired Orin's adventurous streak and laidback approach to life.

It was Orin who first recognized the potential in Nicholas' violin skills and quirky charisma. He persuaded Nicholas to start a YouTube channel, wanting to share his partner's talents with the world. Thrilled by Orin's faith in him, Nicholas eagerly agreed. And so, Nicocado Avocado was born.

At first, the channel was a humble endeavor - just Nicholas casually chatting and playing music in his signature whimsical style. But the earnest content soon garnered a small following. With Orin's encouragement, Nicholas began expanding the videos to share more of his life.

The channel exploded when Nicholas started incorporating mukbangs - filming himself eating large vegan meals on camera. Viewers were drawn to his over-the-top expressions and unfiltered honesty. Seemingly overnight, Nicholas went from an unknown artist to a viral star.

Caught up in the excitement, Nicholas doubled down on outrageous eating challenges to drive more views. The childlike joy he displayed while bingeing on camera resonated with audiences. But privately, a darkness was taking root within Nicholas.

You see, Orin was not the steadfast partner he appeared to be. Behind closed doors, his manipulation and criticism of Nicholas intensified. Orin disapproved of Nicholas' feminine mannerisms and guileless enthusiasm, which he felt embarrassed him.

Isolated and dependent on Orin in a foreign country, Nicholas endured the abusive behavior. He buried his hurt and insecurities in food, gorging on vegan junk food to cope. The more Orin's moods fluctuated, the more Nicholas ate on camera as an outlet.

By late 2016, the relationship was unraveling fast. Orin's verbal and emotional abuse escalated, leaving Nicholas anxious and depressed. In a desperate move to salvage their toxic dynamic, Nicholas proposed to Orin, hoping marriage would bring them closer.

But the engagement only bred more resentment. Orin taunted Nicholas for the proposal, calling it fake and emasculating. His cruel words cut Nicholas to his core, crushing any remaining self-esteem. Nicholas spiraled into a severe depression, turning to food as his only comfort.

The break-up, when it finally came, was almost a relief. No longer beholden to Orin's vitriol, Nicholas fled back to the States in early 2017. But the damage had already been done. Deeply scarred by Orin's manipulation, Nicholas was a shell of himself.

He took refuge in his mukbang channel, now his full-time job. Binging on camera brought the attention he craved, soothing his emotional wounds. But just like his relationship with Orin, Nicholas' addictive behavior was quickly becoming toxic - destroying him from the inside out.

The Allure of Attention

On the surface, Nicholas' YouTube channel appeared wholesome and upbeat. With his playful antics, charming personality, and vegan message, he quickly endeared himself to a loyal audience. But behind the scenes, Nicholas was becoming ensnared by the intoxicating pull of internet fame.

The first taste came after he posted a video venting his frustrations with the vegan community. While he expected backlash, the video instead went viral, garnering Nicholas the most views he'd ever received. For an attention-starved soul like Nicholas, the sudden influx of interest was addictive. It validated his sense of importance and stroked his ego like a drug.

Once Nicholas discovered the power he held to manipulate his audience, a darkness awoke within him. He began deliberately courting controversy, milking his dramatics for views. No longer was it just about spreading a positive message - now Nicholas had an insatiable thirst to be seen.

When he incorporated mukbangs onto his channel, his subscriber count exploded overnight. People were drawn to the perverse spectacle of a dainty, effeminate man gorging on camera. Nicholas fanned the flames, hamming up his reactions and pushing the boundaries with more extreme challenges.

Of course, Nicholas told himself he was just an entertainer, giving the people what they wanted. But in truth, he was locked in a co-dependent relationship with the faceless masses he fed. Their attention was the only thing that could temporarily fill the vast emptiness inside him.

Deep down, Nicholas knew that stuffing his face with junk food was destroying his health. But the instant gratification of views and shock value always won out over common sense. And with every new low he sunk to, his enablers cheered him on - prodding him toward self-destruction for their amusement.

In a tragically ironic twist, Nicholas had become the very thing he once rallied against - a sideshow promoted for profit, not humanity. Only now, instead of external exploiters, Nicholas faced a more sinister oppressor - his own tortured psyche, starved for validation.

Perhaps if he'd had a solid foundation, Nicholas could have withstood fame's corrupting influence. But his fragile self-esteem and lack of purpose made him easy prey. The void within simply redirected his need for connection into a bottomless appetite for attention.

And so began Nicholas' devastating downward spiral. The toxin of internet validation hollowed him out from within, leaving a husk desperate to keep the cameras rolling at any cost. In his fervor to feel seen, Nicholas sacrificed his health, morals and soul - chasing the ephemeral high of cheap fame.

Tragically, the only salvation that could fill Nicholas' inner abyss was the one thing he sought to destroy - a sincere human connection. For no amount of strangers' eyes could compete with the nourishing gaze of someone who truly cared. But in his scramble for validation, Nicholas lost sight of what mattered most. And he would pay dearly for his blindness.

Nicholas' public betrayal of his vegan principles marked a turning point. In a shocking video titled "Why I'm No Longer Vegan," he justified eating meat again as a biological need. Longtime fans felt whiplash from this abrupt shift, accusing Nicholas of selling out.

But the controversy only fueled him. Hungry for attention at any cost, Nicholas ramped up the theatrics, fake crying while woefully proclaiming he didn't want people to hate him. His exaggerated emotions reeled in millions of views, as did his vague allusions to health issues.

Now realizing sensationalism was the path to fame, Nicholas turned his channel into a swirling hive of drama and chaos. Him and his boyfriend Orin became characters in Nicholas' ongoing soap opera, with their volatile relationship as the main storyline.

Nicholas masterfully manipulated his viewers' emotions through this "will they, won't they" dynamic. Each made-up breakup or reconciliation was framed as raw, unfiltered access into Nicholas' inner turmoil. In reality, it was all an act to keep the cameras rolling.

No contrived clickbait stunt was too low for Nicholas now. He poured on the waterworks in videos titles like "This Is NOT Okay" and ranted about Orin's alleged cruelties. Nicholas' exaggerated pain evoked sympathy from his young, gullible fans who couldn't see the deceit.

Addicted to the dizzying highs of viral infamy, Nicholas' content grew more twisted and desperate. He pretended his eye was surgically removed for views, later admitting it was a lie. Nothing was off limits in his relentless pursuit of attention, even fabricating serious health issues.

The innocent, effeminate violinist his fans once adored was gone, replaced by a calculating narcissist drunk on power. Nicholas may have eaten himself to death for the public's entertainment, but their rapt gazes sustained him as much as any food.

In chasing fame, Nicholas sacrificed his soul, selling out his morals for fleeting validation. But the masses kept enabling his downfall, unwilling to look away from the car crash spiraling before them. And caught in the seductive glare of the spotlight, Nicholas came to crave the darkness - for only there did the world truly see him.

Understanding The Game

Here is a draft of the next chapter continuing Nicholas' story:

Chapter 7: A Web of Lies

Nicholas' video lying about his eye removal cemented his willingness to exploit anything for fame - even fabricating serious health conditions. But it was only the beginning of his deceit. Every part of his life now became fodder for sensationalized stories to reel in views.

After the initial proposal video with his boyfriend Orin, Nicholas admitted it was staged. The real proposal had occurred weeks prior, but Nicholas knew a viral moment would bring attention. Nothing was sacred anymore - even intimate moments were exploited.

As the views rolled in, Nicholas seemed untouchable. But his body couldn't keep up with his ravenous hunger for attention. Despite proudly claiming his obesity was "water weight," the fast food was taking its toll.

Nicholas lived in denial, refusing to take accountability for his declining health. He became defensive when fans expressed concern, insisting he was the picture of health no matter how large he grew. But the evidence was clear in each new video - his addictive behavior was slowly killing him.

Desperate for any viral content, Nicholas and Orin even fabricated an entire video about why they broke up, listing times Nicholas had cheated. It was a complete sham, done for shock value and clicks. The once loving couple were now co-conspirators in Nicholas' endless quest for fame, their relationship a mere prop.

After their low-key marriage, Nicholas and Orin held a publicity-stunt ceremony at Chick-fil-A to protest the company's anti-

LGBTQ policies. In reality, it was just another grab at relevance dressed up as activism. Nicholas' principles were long gone - all that remained was an insatiable drive for attention.

By now, Nicholas' act had gotten stale for many longtime fans. His over-the-top personality and constant drama felt inauthentic. But he was trapped, dependent on churning out anything to hold the fickle public's gaze.

So Nicholas clung desperately to relevancy through deception and bile. He abandoned honesty long ago; now his life was a carefully constructed character, distorted for consumption. No healthy relationship could survive in such a toxic ecosystem ruled by lies.

Nicholas lived and breathed for the spotlight's validation. But its harsh glare had long since exposed him as a hollow husk, with no core beneath the flashy exterior. The very thing that sustained him also emptied Nicholas out - until all that remained was a serial fabricator addicted to the next viral high.

After adopting a sloth named Kiwi for content, the animal disappeared from videos shortly after being bitten. Though Nicholas joked he'd eaten it, the truth of Kiwi's fate remained unclear - another dark mystery in Nicholas' twisted world.

Around this time, the health consequences of Nicholas' food addiction became undeniable as his weight ballooned. He pledged to start eating healthy, but unsurprisingly, the effort was short-lived. Nicholas instead blamed his frequent illness on the very diet that could have saved him.

Gone were any pretensions of authenticity - all that remained was Nicholas' insatiable hunger for clicks. He stooped to ever-greater lows, fabricating serious conditions like diabetes and kidney failure for views. Each new deceit seemed to bore Nicholas' dwindling audience more. But by now, he was trapped in the endless feedback loop of shock value.

Things reached a boiling point when Nicholas received news that immigration authorities would soon deport him from Colombia, ending his life there. Though Nicholas spun it as a temporary separation from his husband, in truth, it was the death knell of their dysfunctional relationship.

Having exploited the country for content as long as he could, Nicholas set his sights on returning to America, the holy grail of vapid fame. Back on home turf, his self-destruction could continue feeding the insatiable beast - until he had nothing left to give.

For Nicholas, humanity was just another prop on his path to notoriety. He left chaos and deceit in his wake, alongside broken people, animals and laws. Nothing could stop his reckless stampede toward fame and degradation - not morals, consequences or even his own mortality.

In his depraved stupor, Nicholas forgot that all spectacles must eventually fade. But the internet's memory is long, and his misdeeds would not be so easily buried. The mask was slipping, and beneath it lay the gaping void of a man lost to delusion. But the show would go on, as it always had...at least for now.

An Empire Built on Lunacy

Nicholas' deportation from Colombia marked a sharp descent into full-blown mania. His videos became indistinguishable from deranged performance art, leaving fans questioning his sanity.

Filming himself howling "I'm not having it!" at his reflection, Nicholas embraced unhinged theatrics. His nonsensical outbursts and dialogue with imagined enemies pointed toward a fragmented psyche feasting on its own tail.

Now back in America, his insanity crystallized before rapt followers. To celebrate hitting one million subscribers, Nicholas shaved his head on camera, smearing the remains with egg while sobbing about how no one liked him. Even his most stalwart supporters struggled to comprehend this stunt's purpose beyond perverse titillation.

Yet method lurked in Nicholas' madness - his fixation on numeric milestones revealed a core drive to be seen at scale. And what better place to farther his notoriety than the Florida swamp of clout-chasers? Surrounded by fellow exhibitionists, Nicholas fit right in.

When not engineering public spectacles, Nicholas indulged his gross-out mukbang antics. Footage of him noisily gorging on pungent durian fruit perplexed millions. But their disgust fed Nicholas' growing god complex - he alone decided what was acceptable for the world to witness.

This delusional sense of entitlement metastasized in tandem with his swelling girth. Nicholas bansished words like "healthy" from his comment section, refusing any criticism of his self-destructive methods. He grew irrationally angry at the slightest perception of negativity from fans - their role was to enable his deterioration, not intervene.

But as Nicholas lost touch with reality, his desperation for attention swelled. He picked fights with other internet stars, baiting drama for clicks. Each nonsensical feud provided a Dopamine hit and evidence of his infamy's reach. But the high faded quicker every time, sending Nicholas spiraling further.

The Nicholas his early fans knew was but a distant memory - in his place stood a deranged, narcissistic wreck hellbent on total self-immolation. And yet his insane antics only seemed to draw more eyes. For in his outrageousness lay a twisted mirror reflecting society's latent madness back upon itself.

The more Nicholas flew off the rails, the more venues his mania found for expression. To the young and impressionable, his unhinged persona evinced a dangerous cynicism - proof that sanity was an impediment to fame. But perhaps even this belief too was part of

Nicholas' lunatic theater...for at rock bottom, all lines blur.

Nicholas' stunts took a scatological turn as he mined his toilet habits for content. He nonchalantly vlogged about soiling the bed as his husband remained under the sheets, unfazed by Nicholas' elimination.

Other viral hits included Nicholas shrieking mid-mukbang about defecating himself, before outrageously rubbing his feces into the chair. His fans reacted with disgust, but also fascination at how low Nicholas would sink for attention.

Increasingly immobile from his unchecked eating, Nicholas soon proclaimed he was disabled after injuring his ribs from sneezing. He paraded his new status on camera by using a mobility scooter and sleep apnea mask as props to appear frailer.

Out in public, Nicholas leaned into his provocative persona, hoping to get a rise out of strangers. He'd break into loud flatulence or scream about his uncontrolled diarrhea, relishing the shock value.

For Nicholas, manners and decency were obstacles preventing him from permanently etching his notoriety into the cultural landscape. Only by degrading himself without limits could he attain the anti-fame required to be forever remembered.

This attitude reached its nadir with his disgusting song "Papa's Chicken Sandwich," containing lyrics explicitly describing Nicholas defecating out chicken nuggets in graphic detail. Such unhinged stunts came to define Nicholas' brand, though they left fans puzzled at what was genuine versus performance.

But Nicholas had long abandoned any creative integrity or authenticity. He shamelessly monetized his infamy by charging fans $150 for personalized videos on Cameo. No request was too debased for Nicholas, who willingly demeaned himself for cash to bankroll his dissolute lifestyle.

In surrendering the last shreds of dignity to the all-consuming altar of fame, Nicholas forged his own perverse legacy. Like a disturbed performance artist, he peeled back societal norms to reveal the depravity lurking beneath. And perhaps that was the method within his madness all along – degeneration as revelation, viewed by millions.

Depravity That Knows No Bounds

Nicholas' depraved empire continued expanding like a metastasizing cancer, infecting every corner of the internet with his debauchery. His multitude of YouTube channels formed the dark nucleus at this enterprise's center, pumping out grotesque mukbang videos at a feverish pace.

But the most sinister growths lay on the fringes, where Nicholas exploited society's taboos for profit. On his Patreon page, deranged fans paid to watch him gorge nude, his pale folds rippling with each bite. And for an elite clientele, his OnlyFans offered glimpses into depravities so vile they tested the human capacity for revulsion.

Clearly no violation could satisfy Nicholas' urge to shock and titillate. He knew his audience's appetites were as insatiable as his own gluttony. This feedback loop of supply and demand spiraled exponentially, demanding continuously greater extremes to satiate its cravings.

Soon Nicholas was selling everything from his bodily fluids to Skype sessions where nearly any act or fetish could be accommodated for the right price. Nothing was off the table for the right bidder - Nicholas' last scrap of dignity had long since been devoured.

Somewhere beneath this mountain of quivering flesh and moral decay lay the faint echoes of a passionate young artist. But that flicker of humanity had been smothered under an avalanche of food and fear - fear of obscurity, of being left empty and unseen.

For in Nicholas' warped mind, selling out was noble martyrdom, whoring himself for fame. Only by demolishing every last barrier between impulse and act could he etch his name into eternity as the ultimate counter-icon - hedonism's high priest.

But Nicholas' faith was false - he chased the illusion of fulfillment through destruction. And with each new self-inflicted wound, the voids within him swelled, consuming Nicholas from inside out. Soon this externalized emptiness would devour him completely, leaving behind only a cautionary tale of greed and mania.

Yet perhaps even this was a part of Nicholas' plan - to become so profane as to rivet the masses' attention beyond death. For infamy still held power - the power to sear one's name into humanity's memory beyond mortality. And in the end, to be remembered at all was Nicholas' sole twisted prayer.

At the helm sat his main YouTube channel, which had metastasized into a swarm of subsidiary accounts all dedicated to showcasing Nicholas' insatiable gorging.

With names like Noodle King and More Nikocado, each new channel provided another vector for Nicholas' voracious ego to spread its viral load. Together they formed a multi-headed hydra endlessly churning out vile content. The beast had to be continuously fed - and Nicholas was happy to offer his body as sacrifice.

Nothing was off limits as Nicholas sought new ways to commodify his dissolution. He knew there existed a rabid niche audience who craved access to his total debasement behind the scenes. And so long as the market hungered, Nicholas was happy to feed it his dignity.

In his single-minded pursuit of notoriety, the line between performance and reality had long since blurred. Nicholas constructed alternate personas to fulfill each depraved fantasy - the gluttonous exhibitionist, the flatulent invalid, the sex object glazed in filth.

These fragmented identities allowed Nicholas to dissociate from the horrors he willingly committed upon himself and broadcast to the world. It was auto-voyeurism taken to its logical extreme - Nicholas peering in as his body was defiled from every angle for fame.

Perhaps deep down, some last faint light of conscience still flickered inside Nicholas' darkness. His elaborate role-play provided a protective barrier insulating some small part of his soul from utter damnation. Or maybe this was merely another of narcissism's defenses, constructing lies to obscure the obvious - that nothing human remained.

For in his quest to infect every screen, Nicholas sacrificed his humanity to become a vessel for society's unchecked appetite. Here was the logical conclusion to our age of excess - a man voluntarily demolishing himself to feed the insatiable void of anonymous users. And perhaps that was Nicholas' truest self-offering after all - a warning of gluttony's cost consumed by millions.

Even amidst the mounting distortions, some last vestiges of Nicholas' humanity occasionally peeked through the vulgar facade. One such rare moment came when he grandly announced his purchase of a lavish $2 million penthouse.

Giddy as a child on Christmas, Nicholas gleefully led viewers on a tour of his new palace of excess. The absurd contrast between his decrepit appearance and opulent digs highlighted the surreal nature of his predicament.

Here was a man literally eating himself to death, yet living in the lap of luxury afforded by that very self-destruction. The layers of irony were thick as the grime likely coating Nicholas' new Italian marble floors after an uncensored mukbang.

And for once, Nicholas seemed blissfully unaware of the tragicomedy at play. He was simply a giddy, nouveau-riche showman revealing his glittering kingdom to an adoring public. The filters and theatre were stripped back, allowing Nicholas' innocent enthusiasm to briefly shine through.

Of course, this respite was just an illusion within Nicholas' bigger delusion. But it offered a glimpse into the person he may have been, had kinder circumstances allowed his sensitive spirit to flourish. In another life, he could have filled lavish halls with music and laughter, not depraved spectacle.

But this was not that world. Here, his effusive joy was inextricably linked to self-destruction - the penthouse merely a gilded prison and perch for further egomania. Its pristine chambers would soon be converted into Nicholas' personal carnival of carnage, offering front row seats to his complete undoing.

Still, for this one ephemeral moment, the dreamer buried underneath it all broke free - eyes alight with wonder, unburdened by the insatiable void devouring him from within. Even Nicholas couldn't fully suppress the last fading echoes of innocence below the layers of corruption.

But this salvo of light made the surrounding darkness feel more ominous. For it confirmed a soul still flickered within the smothering folds - meaning Nicholas had made a choice to destroy himself in service of his delusions. Somewhere beneath this baroque palace lay a man who once dreamt of joy, not ravishment on a global stage.

Perhaps that man watched from inside, peering out through Nicholas' eyes, seeing the world but powerless to change course. If so, then this was his last wistful gasp of hope before the end. A final twinkle of humanity before the curtain fell on Nicholas' humanity for good.

Rage and Ruin

Amidst the gluttony and spectacle, one aspect of Nicholas' persona loomed largest in public imagination - his explosive temper. Violent mood swings had become a signature of his unhinged brand, eagerly anticipated by rubbernecking fans.

At the slightest annoyance, Nicholas morphs into a shrieking banshee, his world-class tantrums akin to an oversized toddler. What deeply disturbs is the authentic fury his face displays in these moments - eyes wild with rage, spittle flying, face contorted incapacitating malice.

The triviality of the triggers makes his deranged reaction all the more unsettling. A stray cat being fed outside his window unleashes a category 5 meltdown. Botched food orders elicit profanity-laced diatribes. All captured for viral infamy.

For devoted followers, waiting for the next detonation of Mount Nikocado became a grotesque spectator sport. Bookies could have set odds on what innocuous comment or event would set him off next. But while fans viewed the blowups as entertainment, they evinced a profound disturbance within Nicholas.

This was not typical anger, but unhinged madness waiting to burst forth at any moment. His psyche had become a pressure cooker always threatening to explode, unless constantly pacified with food and attention. Any dissent immediately transformed Nicholas into a writhing ball of rage.

Perhaps this rage arose from the conflicts between his persona and true self. The outward exhibitionist clashed with the sensitive soul trapped underneath, constantly provoking turmoil. Or maybe it was withdrawal from the dopamine hits of fame.

Whatever the cause, these fits illuminated Nicholas' lack of control over his existence. He was hostage to compulsions he could scarcely comprehend, let alone restrain. And so he continued lashing out - at the world, at loved ones, at himself. An embodiment of fury chanting into the void, slowly extinguishing the light within.

For Nicholas had become a man at war with himself, driven to destroy the very things that once brought him joy. Each vicious outburst was another battle in that endless internal conflict between who Nicholas was and what he had let himself become. Until all that remained was a shell - angry, empty and alone.

A Toxic Bond

Nicholas was not the only one transformed beyond recognition during his public unraveling. His husband Orin had also morphed from a supportive partner into a bitter, henpecking spouse.

Where once stood a calm, kind soul now raged a petty tyrant, hurling cruel barbs at Nicholas constantly. Their exchanges dripped with vitriol - Orin mocking Nicholas as a "dumpster fire" and "walking meme." This contempt seemed to fill some sadistic need in Orin, even as it clearly pained his husband.

In fairness, Orin had witnessed firsthand the ways fame had corroded Nicholas' character. His husband was no longer the man he loved - just a narcissistic shell desperate for attention. Orin's resentment was the bitterness of dreams dashed and affection betrayed.

But Orin stayed, either bound by marriage vows or simply resigned to the circus. Their toxic dynamic played out before addicted viewers, prodding the death spiral onward. Orin's meanness gave Nicholas license to act out more, feeding the beast of cheap drama.

Yet hints of their old tenderness occasionally surfaced between barbs, suggesting some faint ember of love yet smoldered under the ashes. Both remained trapped in roles fate had laid for them - Nicholas a court jester gorging desperately; Orin the heckler goading him toward oblivion.

Perhaps Orin's mockery was also tinged with a sadistic mercy - an attempt to hasten the end of Nicholas' debasement before he lost himself completely. Either way, their once-strong bond had become just another tether tying Nicholas to his staged persona. Too much history bound them together to permit escape.

Both men were shackled to this slow-motion disaster, relegated to playing caricatures of themselves. With each nasty exchange, another layer of authentic humanity peeled away, leaving behind only calcified anger and regret. Where once bloomed the tender flower of new love, now remained only thorns.

Yet even this mutually destructive partnership evinced a certain nihilistic devotion - two souls bound by trauma, reflecting one another's damage until all wounds fused into a single scar. A part of them would always remain entwined, even if only by shared resistance to healing old scars. For that, a kind of love endured.

Trouble in Mukbang Paradise

For a brief moment, it seemed Nicholas had found kinship with fellow mukbangers Stephanie Soo and Zach Choi. Their collab videos were jovial affairs, with the trio laughing and indulging together. But behind the scenes, tensions were mounting that would erupt dramatically.

In a bombshell video, Stephanie accused Nicholas of manipulative and predatory behavior. She claimed he pressured her into collaborations and used personal information to intimidate her. Fearing for her safety, Stephanie exposed his alleged abuses publicly.

The accusations detonated like a bomb, unleashing a mushroom cloud of outrage across the internet. Nicholas was swiftly tried and convicted in the court of public opinion. Allegations of bullying and harassment engulfed comment sections. Once again, he was a pariah.

When Nicholas finally responded, he appeared genuinely bewildered by the allegations. He denied any ill intent, offering reasonable explanations for the incidents cited. But by then, the damage was done. Most fans refused to believe his side of the story.

In truth, the reality likely lay somewhere in a gray area, a messy misunderstanding between complicated personalities. But nuance stood no chance in the age of snap judgments and callout bloodlust. Nicholas was branded a villain, with dissenting opinions shouted down.

Both parties probably harbored some culpability. But only one faced righteous mob wrath. For Nicholas, this was yet another harsh lesson in the fickle nature of online fame. One day a cheeky anti-hero, the next a canceled cretin. Forgiveness was not this generation's strong suit.

The saga illustrated the warped interpersonal dynamics that develop on

YouTube. Relationships are transactional, notoriety the ultimate currency. Bonds form and fracture based on fickle metrics of viewership and controversy. Trust becomes collateral damage.

Perhaps for brief moments, a real friendship existed between these lonely souls using food and screens to fill inner voids. But in the funhouse mirror world of virtual interactions, even good intentions soon twist into suspicion. For connection without humanity is but a hollow parody.

Another hollow spectacle for viewers to inevitably forget. But for those involved, the damage was lasting - their brief bond severed, innocence lost.

The fallout from Stephanie Soo was just one in a string of dramas that became Nicholas' new sustenance. Lurching from feud to feud kept him relevant as his actual content stagnated into repetition. But it came at a cost to his humanity.

Each new clash further cemented his reputation as an unhinged villain, consorting with darkness for kicks. But the real darkness stemmed from a gnawing emptiness inside Nicholas that fame could never satisfy. So he chased increasingly extreme provocation to fill the void.

When his OnlyFans content spread across Twitter, Nicholas reacted with deranged glee, threatening more vulgar antics. But behind the bluster was a profound humiliation - his boundaries violated, body autonomy destroyed. Reduced to a laughing stock, his sense of self further unraveled.

A pattern emerged - Nicholas would provoke controversy, the internet would retaliate disproportionately, then Nicholas would retaliate again, ad infinitum. Both sides convinced their cause was just, oblivious to the spectacle they were performing. Like opposing reflections in a hall of mirrors, the truth was obscured.

Perhaps on some level Nicholas understood that each feud fueled his infamy. But the short-term thrill eclipsed any thought for long-term consequences. All that mattered was sustaining the dizzying high, avoiding the crash.

So Nicholas continued his manic dance with the furies, lashing out at critics and enabling their most sadistic impulses. Two distorted parts locked in co-dependent mania, both complicit in their mutual destruction. For Nicholas had become not just spectacle, but manifestation of the internet's hunger for outrage.

In devouring others, he hoped to avoid being devoured himself. But with each new battle, Nicholas sacrificed more of his soul, becoming the very darkness he fought. For no matter how voracious, this appetite could never be filled from the outside in. The void could only be filled by looking within. Until then, the cycle would continue - a snake eating its own tail, trapped in an endless feedback loop of empty hunger.

In the aftermath of the Stephanie Soo saga, Nicholas' hunger for conflict only grew more insatiable. Lurching from one feud to the next became his new form of self-harm, eliciting a dopamine rush more potent than any food high.

Fueled by narcissistic rage, he lashed out against critics and former friends alike. Each new battle further cemented his reputation as an unhinged villain, but Nicholas was intoxicated by the notoriety. In his twisted mind, infamy equaled influence.

When his OnlyFans content spread across Twitter like wildfire, Nicholas reacted with deranged glee, threatening more vulgar stunts to stoke the flames. But behind the bluster was a profound humiliation – his boundaries violated, autonomy destroyed. Reduced to a laughing stock, his last shreds of dignity disintegrated.

Yet Nicholas couldn't stop himself from prodding the hornet's nest, provoking exactly the mistreatment that wounded him most. Trapped in a masochistic cycle, he became both abuser and abused, simultaneously desperate for validation and determined to destroy anyone who gave it.

For Nicholas was ruled not by conscience, but impulse. His emotional regulation was that of a child, lashing out blindly when hurt or frustrated. Each new battle offered a fresh dopamine surge to sustain him through the inevitable comedown. Around and around the carousel spun.

In some ways, he had become the embodiment of digital pathology - reckless, reactionary, constantly performing for invisible masses. Forged in isolation and raised on pixels, he lacked the tools to disengage. The only mode he knew was attack and escalation. There could be no peace when addiction ruled.

Of course, the masses were equally complicit, prodding Nicholas on at every turn. His outbursts entertained them, offering welcome catharsis for modern resentments. Together, provocateur and audience locked in a dysfunctional waltz, stoking humanity's worst instincts in each other.

And so Nicholas spiraled further down the abyss of spectacle, sacrificing more of his soul with each new outrage. Yet the fleeting high always evaporated, leaving him emptier than before. For no amount of external toxins could fill the hollowness within him. Until that void was addressed, the hunger would remain.

Lost in the Spectacle

Amidst the endless spectacle, it was perhaps inevitable that real tragedy would eventually pierce Nicholas' reality bubble. When a woman's distant screams rang out during one mukbang, neither he nor Orin reacted, lost in their banal chatter.

Only later did implications arise - a deadly stabbing had allegedly occurred in Nicholas' building that night. If true, this lent chilling context to their indifference. Desensitized by theatrics, real horror barely registered through the haze.

Ironically, it was Nicholas' regular viewers who flagged the unnerving moment, jolted by its contrast to the usual vulgar burlesque. For many, it highlighted the numbing effects of his videos' constant bombast. Outrage defenses were now on hair-trigger, reality blurred.

Soon Nicholas proposed submitting his footage to aid the hypothetical murder investigation, his content gaining new purpose. But ethical questions lingered about consent and exploitation. True crime had become just another of Nicholas' genres, the woman's cries fodder for re-analysis.

Perhaps for Nicholas, the sounds simply melded into the surrounding cacophony that characterized his daily life. Screams, flatulence, weeping - it was all track layers in the ongoing opera documenting his breakdown. Sustained sensory overload had dulled his instincts for what mattered.

In this, Nicholas was less an anomaly than a pioneer experiencing the dystopian endgame of online anarchy firsthand. For when attention is lifeblood, moral sanity unravels. Eyes stay locked on the spectacle, however dark.

But we too are accountable for normalizing Nicholas' numbing excesses. A media machine built to stoke outrage has little incentive for restraint. Provocateurs rise up to meet demand. Standards erode gradually, imperceptibly, until the grotesque defines the age.

So where is the line? When does drama become exploitation? What does it say about society when a woman's dying cries are just another plot point in the 24-hour content churn? In the end, creator and spectator shape each other, locked in co-dependent waltz. And perhaps the line between was always gossamer thin.

For we all crave distraction from private voids. And in Nicholas' bizarre frolics, many glimpse dark desires of rebellion and abandon reflected back at them. To denounce his dissolution, society must confront its own. But that requires more courage than simply watching the car crash unfold.

Reflections in the Mirror

Stepping back, Nicholas' saga evokes a complex range of reactions. On one hand, the garish theatrics repel - who would degrade themselves so publicly, if not mentally unwell? But morbid fascination lingers, even in the most skeptical. What does our collective rubbernecking say about society's darkness?

Some label Nicholas a genius playing the system - architect of his infamy. But genius implies foresight and control, while Nicholas exhibits neither, chained to compulsions he can scarcely understand. He is no mastermind, just mastered.

Nor is he simply "mentally ill" in the clinical sense. Dark appetites lurk within all minds; most simply restrain them. Nicholas' mania reflects suppressed shadow desires of millions, given permission to manifest completely. He is id unchained.

In truth, Nicholas was forged by the internet's fire into his current grotesque effigy. His audience's appetite for extremity evoked a performer to meet that craving. Their gazes warped him, as his theatrics corrupted their sensibilities in turn. A hall of mirrors, where cause and effect circle endlessly.

Perhaps at the start, some shred of shrewd opportunism guided Nicholas down the path of sensationalism. But he tread unaware of the Faustian bargain it required. For fame'spreprocessor demands all - self-respect, health, sanity - leaving a gnawing void.

And so Nicholas spiraled, sculpting his persona to feed the internet's endless hunger. But its malignant energy twisted him into a hideous parody of humanity, bound by mania and needing eyes at any cost. For better or worse, he had become the monster his audience desired.

This is both Nicholas' defense and his indictment - his dissolution was driven by crowds thirsting for darkness. But he also chose appeasement over resistance, a short-lived fortune over lasting dignity. His culpability lies in acquiescence, not inception.

For we all have shadow parts yearning to run free - to eat, sin and smear oneself in filth for applause. But most heed the inner voice warning that no price is worth losing one's soul. Tragically, when offered fame's fruits, Nicholas silenced his conscience and fed the beast within us all.

And so in gazing voyeuristically at Nicholas, we behold our secret demons reflected back in the extreme. The line between participant and spectator blurs. We are complicit in the masquerade so many condemn. For Nicholas is merely a mirror - the rest is up to us.

At times, Nicholas drops his histrionic facade, offering glimpses of humanity behind the caricature. In candid moments, his genuine warmth and talent shine through, evoking the person he could have been without the internet's corrupting glare.

When he expresses hopes to get healthy or repairs things with his husband, we witness fleeting redemption. But the machinations are stronger, always dragging Nicholas back into the mire. For momentary sincerity garners less attention than garish spectacle.

So the dramatics resume - exaggerated breakups, scandals, quitting and binging in endless permutation. Nicholas continues publicly imploding, leaving fragmented identities and broken relationships in his wake.

Yet one senses exhaustion creeping in. The perpetual cycle of bingeing and purging for attention has depleted Nicholas. Even his anger seems now ritualized, the last sputtering of a dying star.

At times, behind the forced smile, sincere sorrow pierces through - regret at squandering his potential for fleeting infamy; mourning dreams foregone and principles abandoned. Somewhere beneath the layers of affectation, Nicholas' inner light still flickers, however dimly.

Perhaps this is the greatest tragedy - that behind the grotesque facade lurks the ghostly outline of someone sensitive and talented, never fully obscured. It is the perpetual disconnect between his soul's true longing and the appetites he forces it to feed that generates such profound self-loathing.

For Nicholas chose his path, and culpability remains. But there is also pathos in witnessing a good nature systematically destroyed from within and without. And part of us still hopes the prodigal mukbanger may complete his cycle of degradation and seek redemption before it's too late.

But that choice belongs to Nicholas alone. Should he find the courage to cast off artifice and live sincerely, forgiveness awaits. Until then, the masquerade continues, and so too does our collective complicity in sustaining it. For in funding the spectacle, we grant it power over us.

Weight Loss Revisited – Hope, Perhaps?

As 2023 dawned, Nicholas unveiled plans to reclaim his health with a rigorous weight loss program. After years of self-destructive binge eating, he pledged to overhaul his lifestyle and lose weight through diet and exercise.

Initially, Nicholas' optimism was contagious. He spoke of hiring coaches, cooking healthy meals, and adopting a consistent workout regimen. For once it seemed he was taking personal responsibility rather than relying on spectacle.

Fans lauded his initiative, heartened to see this first step toward redemption. The early videos were hopeful - documenting modest improvements as Nicholas stuck to his regimen. Though wary of getting their hopes up, longtime viewers allowed cautious optimism.

The first weeks brought visible progress as the pounds slowly began to shed. Nicholas posted grateful updates thanking supporters for keeping him motivated. Their positive reinforcement fueled his new commitment to bettering himself.

For the first time in ages, Nicholas appeared driven by genuine growth rather than just chasing shock value. His content reflected harmony and balance rather than dysfunction. It was as if the old Nicholas many came to love was finally re-emerging.

Of course, whether this initial promise would last was uncertain. But for now, Nicholas seemed on the right path, having realized his destructive patterns were untenable. After so much darkness, his supporters found solace in this glimmer of light. For once, the future looked bright.

Whatever lay ahead, this moment was one of hope - Nicholas standing bravely at the crossroads choosing health and wholeness. Only time would tell where that road ultimately led. But for now, the journey had begun, step by promising step.

Glimpses of Clarity

Amidst the theatrics, Nicholas occasionally reveals his more reflective side, such as in his epic 2-hour rebuttal against a vegan teacher who criticized him. Dropping his online persona, Nicholas addresses her claims with unexpected nuance.

Gone is the unhinged provocateur, replaced by someone articulate and incisive. With lawyerly precision, he dismantles her distortions with facts and reason. For those accustomed to his histrionics, this Nicholas is almost unrecognizable.

Yet his passionate advocacy reveals flashes of his former vegan self - still grounded in ethics, just overshadowed by mania. In these moments of clarity, the sensibilities that once moved him to activism emerge from the fog.

Some may question this earnest version of Nicholas, deeming it another fabrication. But the shift seems authentic, more engaged debate than entertainment. For the first time in ages, substance takes priority over spectacle.

Of course, the lucidity is relative, sandwiched between digressions into conspiracy theories and dubious medical claims. But his core arguments hold up well under scrutiny, giving lie to notions that he lacks intelligence or conviction.

The implications are stark - behind the cartoonish buffoonery lies an articulate person whose inner light has been obscured, but not fully extinguished. This hints at the potential redemption awaiting should he re-align with his higher values.

For all have inner contradictions - wisdom and compulsion competing for influence. At his best, Nicholas models reconciliation of these disparate drives, channeling emotions constructively rather than destructively. But these moments are fleeting.

Still, the flashes of insight offer hope. They suggest that beneath the layers of corruption festering at his core, Nicholas' soul persists, however compromised. And where life remains, change stays possible. But the choice rests with him.

Though the circus may continue for now, this version of Nicholas represents the road not taken - principled, deliberate, humane. Should he choose to walk it, that path remains open. But first he must silence the ringmaster who holds the whip. Only he can decide if redemption is worth abandoning the spectacle.

Amidst fraught relationships, Nicholas found surprising chemistry with fellow mukbanger Hungry Fat Chick. Their collaborations reveal two kindred spirits using food and spectacle to fill inner voids.

In videos together, a bizarre sincerity emerges between the gluttony and theatrics. Bound by trauma and compulsion, they take solace in each other's company without judgment. For once, Nicholas seems at ease - his guard lowered, eccentricities embraced.

Laughing freely, the pair indulge in childlike antics, like measuring their widening girth before gorging on noodles. For all its grotesqueness, a genuine affection comes through. An oasis of acceptance in their otherwise hostile world.

This bond evinces the inherent contradictions of Nicholas' path. While fame and degradation have cost him so much, they have also granted him community with fellow outcasts. In the margins, beyond societal norms, Nicholas has found his niche.

Yet there is tragedy even in this - for the only place he found belonging was among those as damaged as himself. His connections were forged through self-destruction and denigration, not mutual care or virtue. Still, some solace endures.

Seeing Nicholas drop his cynical persona to interact with openness and humor hints at the man buried below the layers of corruption. It suggests that beneath the monster façade lies a sensitive soul seeking connection, however warped its expression.

This is the central paradox of Nicholas' plight - his humanity persists, yet is continually subsumed by his monstrous compulsions. Again and again, those fleeting luminous moments are devoured by the insatiable darkness.

Only Nicholas can resolve this struggle within himself. His redemption lies in elevating those redeeming traits - empathy, authenticity, creativity - and shedding the traits that debase him and sever bonds.

Glimmers of Progress

After months of promising but sporadic effort, a shift occurred in Nicholas' weight loss journey. In a shocking video, he appeared noticeably slimmer, claiming a dubious 89 pound loss. Nicholas seemed almost cheerful and at peace.

His demeanor was equally surprising. None of the histrionic theatrics or binges - just Nicholas calmly enjoying a meal with his husband. He spoke with upbeat self-awareness about his progress, rather than making outrageous claims.

For skeptical longtime viewers, his transformation seemed almost too good to be true. But the sincerity came through in the video's thoughtful quality and Nicholas' relaxed joy. This was not clickbait - it felt like real change.

Perhaps after hitting rock bottom emotionally, Nicholas had finally committed to redemption. His supporters rejoiced at this apparent breakthrough. Though still wary of false hope, they couldn't help but celebrate what looked like rebirth.

Seeing Nicholas and Orin reconnect over an earnest meal strengthened the sense this was a new chapter. Amidst their playful banter shone real closeness - the nonsense and toxicity stripped away. It was a glimpse into the relationship that first brought them together.

Of course, whether this shift would last was uncertain. But the video offered the first concrete hope that Nicholas could be restored to wholeness. For once, the motivations seemed intrinsic, not just chasing viewership and shock value.

Time would tell if Nicholas would backslide into old patterns. But this moment provided touching assurance that beneath everything, his true spirit endured. With sustained care and discipline, perhaps it could be coaxed into the light once more.

For now, skepticism was set aside to appreciate this tender sapling of redemption. After so much anguish, Nicholas had gifted the world a rare spark of inspiration. For if someone so lost could find his way, hope lived on for us all.

In recent months, intriguing shifts have occurred in Nicholas' content. While still dabbling in spectacle, more videos show him out of character, suggesting legitimate lifestyle changes.

On his secondary channel, candid weigh-ins document modest weight loss, though the journey remains in its early phases. Nicholas seems aware that keeping viewers means occasionally donning the provocateur's mask - but it no longer defines him.

When the theatrics drop, a thoughtful earnestness emerges. During cooking videos with Orin, their playful rapport reflects a reconcilement. Gone is the toxicity and turmoil - now they collaborate with endearing clumsiness.

Seeing Nicholas embrace traditional domestic pursuits shows a man slowly rediscovering passions beyond food and drama. While still utilizing his notoriety, he appears less consumed by the void it was meant to fill. There is a sense of progress at work.

Of course, skepticism remains warranted. But the grains of subtler humanity suggest Nicholas is charting a path beyond his warped persona. The volatility and fury are dampening, his outlook increasingly introspective.

This is not wholesale reinvention - the attention addiction and showmanship persist. But they share space with self-awareness and accountability now. It is the early stirring of a soul seeking equilibrium.

Where this newfound balance leads remains unclear. Perhaps the demons will override again, plunging Nicholas back into extremes. But for now, a glimmer of hope endures. Where there is life, redemption stays possible. The next chapter has yet to be written.

For Nicolas and all who have strayed far from the path, the door is never fully shut. Through compassion and courage, one step leads to the next until wholeness is in sight once more.

The Price of Provocation

For every video where Nicholas drops the theatrics, he releases another dripping in toxicity. Case in point - "Why We Can't Break Up," disliked over 46,000 times for its cruel dynamic with Orin.

The contrast with his thoughtful cooking video is jarring. Here the playful Nicholas is gone, replaced by a bitter spouse relentlessly mocking and belittling Orin. Each barb intended to emotionally wound, met only with pained resignation.

This is the Nicholas that makes fans question his humanity - a bully prodding a helpless victim purely for spectacle. The callousness serves no purpose beyond riling up controversy and clicks. It is narcissism devoid of empathy.

And yet the rewards are clear - 3.4 million views fueled by outrage, morbid fascination and partisan takes. Nicholas may pay the price in reputation, but the bank account swells. The cost to his soul is harder to quantify.

Perhaps these vicious displays offer a window into Nicholas' inner self-loathing, projected outward as vitriol. Or maybe they are merely a cynical pantomime to keep eyes locked on the car crash. The motives are layered and opaque.

But the impact is clearer - each video like this further warps Nicholas' psyche and erodes his supporters' goodwill. The poison seeps in for all involved - creator, enablers, gawkers. None emerge unscathed.

For Nicholas, it sets up a vicious cycle - outrage brings views but destroys spirit. Persona battles true self until neither recognizes the other. Bad faith drives out good, leaving a void where humanity once dwelled.

So while being cruel makes commercial sense, Nicholas pays a stealthier price - his mind, eroded by malice. And once that damage is done, redemption becomes costlier. But Nicholas has always played the short game, focused on the next viral hit.

Perhaps one day he will tire of outrage, seek meaning over money. But for now, provocation and spite pay the bills. Though profitable, this path propels him further from inner peace. In the end, the true cost is beyond any ledger's accounting.

The Eye of the Storm

This summer brought an unexpected respite in Nicholas' barrage of content. For the first time in ages, his channels went silent as he took an unannounced hiatus in June. After years of nonstop spectacle, what prompted this sudden withdrawal?

For longtime followers, the break elicited cautious optimism. Perhaps, like an addict seeking rehab, Nicholas had finally hit rock bottom and recognized the need for help. His health and relationships were disintegrating - had he chosen to intervene before it was too late?

His motivation for quitting remained opaque. But the tangible benefits were soon apparent. Metrics showed his earnings held steady despite the lack of new uploads. For once, Nicholas' absence did not financially impact him - the juggernaut rolled on.

This revelation may have granted an epiphany - that he no longer needed to destroy himself daily to maintain his lifestyle. The machine he built now ran without him. For the first time in ages, he could step back.

Of course, skepticism endures about what ultimately motivated the hiatus. But for a brief moment, the cacophony went silent. The gale winds halted, the waves calmed. It was the eye of the storm - a chance for introspection before the maelstrom resumed.

Perhaps in the stillness, glimpses of reality pierced Nicholas' distorted perceptions. Perhaps old dreams long buried stirred once more. Or maybe the break changed nothing, just a blip before the next outrage.

But we celebrate rest when it comes, whether permanent or fleeting. For living sensibly is Nicholas' greatest rebellion against the forces that propel his mania. Where the eye passes, hope endures of calmer seas ahead. The weeks to come will reveal all.

The Façade Starts To Crumble

Nicholas' unexplained disappearance left fans grasping for answers. Insight finally came from an unlikely source - his husband Orlin, in a video titled "Why Nick Quit YouTube." According to Orlin, Nicholas' stalled weight loss progress had spurred a mental health crisis.

As Orlin tells it, Nicholas had grown despondent after his initial weight loss plateaued. Unable to maintain discipline, he would binge violently, erasing any progress. Each failed attempt left him more depressed and self-loathing, until he finally quit YouTube in despair.

Of course, skepticism looms over this version of events. Orlin's take is likely distorted by his own biases and questionable motives. Perhaps the break had simpler reasons - exhaustion, a genuine vacation, strategic planning.

Yet even if the details are murky, Orlin's video revealed cracks in Nicholas' carefully constructed facade. After years of projecting success and stability, the reality of his inner turmoil emerged. The upheaval called everything into question.

If Orlin's claims rang even partially true, it signified Nicholas' misery had finally superseded his drive for fame. For years, he chased the spectacle despite self-destruction. Now, perhaps the pain grew too acute to ignore.

Some speculate the break was a last-ditch effort to salvage his health before it was too late. A moment of clarity about the price of his pursuit. If so, it came none too soon. But easy fixes seldom exist for ones so lost.

Whatever the impetus, for the first time consequences seemed to penetrate Nicholas' mania in a meaningful way. His indifference to the damage gave way, if only temporarily, to the human reality beneath the caricature. A revelation awaited there, should he choose to see it.

But Nicholas' next steps remain uncertain. Will he learn from this rupture in his programming, or brush it off and plunge forward once more? For now, the façade has cracked. But real change takes courage few can muster when backed against the wall. The true test is yet to come.

Another Glimpse Of Hope

Nicholas' return to YouTube brought another surprising shift - in a new video entitled "How Much I Weigh," the provocateur persona was once again absent. Instead, an earnest Nicholas cooked and bantered lightheartedly with Orlin.

Their easy rapport evidenced a reconciliation during the break. minor spats arose, but Nicholas quickly diffused any dramatic escalation. The toxicity that once defined their collabs was dialed back, allowing genuine affection to emerge.

Once again fans responded positively, much preferring this version of Nicholas. The drama and outbursts felt stale - people yearned to see the real person behind the clownish facade. This video offered a taste, hinting at who Nicholas was beyond the spectacle.

The contrast illustrates why Nicholas' channel exploded initially - his effusive personality and passion for life. Before the nonstop gluttony and breakdowns, he won over audiences with his genuineness. Amidst the chaos, that earnest soul still peeked through.

Of course, the profitability of provocation seemed to preclude a permanent return to form. But the glimmers of humanity gave supporters hope that reconciliation with himself remained possible. Perhaps the glimpses could become the norm rather than aberration.

For no matter how severe the sickness, remnants of one's essential character persist. Life events may distort the personality, but the spirit endures. For Nicholas, the road back to himself was long - but scenes like these suggested the path remained open, should he decide to walk it.

True redemption requires more than a video - it necessitates a fundamental change within. But the most arduous journeys begin with a flicker of longing for wisdom and wellness. If Nicholas could sustain that flicker, fanning it to a flame, then hope lived.

The Cycle Resumes

The positivity of Nicholas' return proved short-lived. Soon attention-grabbing antics resumed, evidenced by videos like "10,000 Calorie Noodle Challenge" that opened with flatulence. This ticked all the boxes for lowbrow clickbait, and views followed.

But the cost was clear in the torrent of downvotes and scathing comments. Most fans had hoped the brief glimpses of humanity presaged something more. But once again, spectacle took priority over substance.

Collaborations with Hungry Fat Chick followed a similar trajectory. After showing promise with lighthearted cooking, Nicholas dove into enabling gluttony once more. Their weigh-ins attracted particular ire, seen as undermining Candy's weight loss.

The pattern grew predictable - provocative concepts drew clicks but eroded Nicholas' goodwill steadily. Each attempt to walk the line between authenticity and sensationalism failed, skewing ever more towards the latter. In the end, the beast must be fed.

The most recent videos elicit a feeling of resignation - that no matter how many times Nicholas shows potential for change, the compulsions win out. He remains trapped in the cycle of brief self-awareness inevitably drowned out by mania.

Perhaps one day the pattern will finally break and a permanent shift occur. But the inertia of years is not easily overcome. And the internet's incentives remain unchanged - scandal brings eyeballs, integrity is quantified.

For Nicholas and creators like him, the battle is constant between lower drives and higher purpose. Every day brings an existential choice - feed the void with whatever sustains the metrics, or nourish the soul with meaning. One promises transient thrills, the other lasting fulfillment.

Which road Nicholas takes remains his choice. But his growing ennui hints he may be tiring of the cycle - seeking more than momentary highs. All lost souls desire connection and purpose deep down. For Nicholas, the path is there when he is ready to see it. The rest unfolds day by day.

After showing real progress moderating his content and lifestyle, this relapse into extremes rang hollow. Supporters felt whiplash from the abrupt reversal after a period of hope. It seemed the brief glimmers of humanity were fleeting - the beast must always be fed.

Hungry Fat Chick's own regression added to the sense of dismay. She had been succeeding on her weight loss journey, only to abandon it due to waning views. A vicious cycle thus ensued - declining engagement led creators to sacrifice integrity and destroy their health chasing clicks.

In collaborating, Nicholas and Candy enabled each other's worst compulsions. Their excessive feast left supporters crestfallen rather than titillated. The ensuing backlash was a harbinger - audiences were tiring of the circus. The antics that once shocked now felt sadly predictable.

For Nicholas, this cooling of interest presented a reckoning. The old bag of tricks was becoming ineffective, requiring ever more outlandish stunts just to maintain views. Chasing this dopamine would only lead further down the rabbit hole.

Now at a crossroads, which path will Nicholas take going forward - continue self-exploiting for fleeting reward or courageously chart a new course centered on creativity and meaning? His restlessness hints the former is losing its luster. But change takes fortitude in face of fear.

The next chapter remains unwritten. But possibilities await should Nicholas rediscover his artistic spirit and leave destruction behind. The internet's eye will wander - but integrity stands the test of time. By looking within, he can yet find the light that leads out of darkness. The choice ahead is his alone.

Stuck in the Spiral

In recent videos, Nicholas has plunged to new nadirs, signaling an irrepressible spiral. As views wane, his stunts grow increasingly twisted in a desperate gambit to recapture attention. But the effect is repellent rather than riveting.

Case in point: a video titled "Eating is My Only Reason to Live" featuring Nicholas erotically tonguing wet noodles. Set to sultry music, the grotesque display evoked derision more than shock value. Fans sensed a performer stripped of all pretense and humanity.

When provocation falls flat, Nicholas doubles down on dysfunction. Public fights with Orlin return frequently, laying bare their broken dynamic. Entreaties to "rescue" Nicholas from the relationship evince deep unease from viewers.

Yet the cycle persists - manufactured drama to stir engagement, however fleeting. The mania is ossifying, diminishing returns requiring ever more unhinged antics just to tread water. But the oblivion approaches stealthily.

Each stunt chips away at the precarious scaffolding holding Nicholas above the abyss, hastening his inevitable crash. With nowhere left to go, he circles the drain faster, lashing out blindly, seeking the next viral spark through degradation.

Here is the tragic denouement of Nicholas' arc - a Icarus who flew too close to the sun, addicted to its gaze. Now having torched his wings, the fall remains - slowed by half measures, but certain. For the dancer and the dance are bound eternally.

This is addiction's final calculus - destroy yourself chasing the diminishing highs before the lights go out for good. And Nicholas is too far gone to accept the ultimate buzzkill - leading a quiet, dignified life. The hunger outweighs the man.

Perhaps one day he will rediscover meaning beyond attention, but today is not that day. As his thresholds keep lowering, humanity slips further away. All that remains is the spiral, accelerating until its host finally burns out. The flames rise higher, hungry still.

Chasing Oblivion

As another year comes to a close, Nicholas' trajectory seems locked into a terminal nosedive. His stunts grow more desperate and viewers more dismayed, yet the cycle persists - a snake devouring itself.

Videos show an alarming disconnect from reality. Nicholas alternates between vitriolic outbursts at Orlin and laughing them off moments later. Disordered thinking overtakes empathy and reason. It is the final unmooring.

When cruel spectacle fails to garner applause, Nicholas stumbles briefly, questioning the false narratives that fuel his mania. But lucidity quickly yields again to lunacy - the drive to self-annihilate overrides all.

Fans witness the externalization of Nicholas' internal dissolution in real time.

The wise turn away, unwilling to enable the decline. But fascination lingers for those who see in Nicholas the personification of their own dark impulses. They will stay tuned till the bitter end.

And Nicholas continues his merry jig toward oblivion, embracing infamy over anonymity, madness over mediocrity. His life becomes ritualized mania - binge, purge, outrage, repeat. Momentary lapses into humanity pass quicker each time before the beast reclaims its host.

For Nicholas, the only way out now is down. Too much time and lifeforce wasted chasing vapidity leave him incapable of pivoting to meaning and self-work. The fear of irrelevance outweighs the fear of self-destruction. So the circus trudges on.

Perhaps one day the clamor will cease and Nicholas will look inward to fill the voids he so desperately ran from. But for now, that day is not this day. There is only the churn, the churn, the churn, numbing him to the precipice. And so Nicholas dances on, enthralled by oblivion's siren song.

The Final Descent

As Nicholas' precipitous downfall accelerated, his world narrowed to a schizophrenic vortex of food and fabrication.Videos from this period documented a psyche unraveling in real time before rapt, uneasy viewers.

Gone were any pretenses of authenticity - now Nicholas inhabited a solipsistic realm where fact and fantasy blurred into a warped burlesque. Manic cycles of binging, public outbursts and reconciliations repeated ad nauseam, eclipsing reality's anchor.

In a rambling video, he alluded to a split with Orlin, claiming they now lived separately. But the next day's post featured them together, as if nothing had occurred. It was gaslighting taken to its extreme end stage - denying lived experiences to replace them with delusion.

Yet Nicholas persisted in proclaiming semi-coherent insights into his own condition, as if hovering above the fray. He acknowledged his penchant for fabrication, but couldn't stop the compulsions steering his life toward disaster. The self still yearned to be known, even as it disappeared.

For his longtime supporters, this period was profoundly unsettling. The Nicholas they had rooted for was gone, consumed by psychosis and carnival spectacle. Many pleaded for him to get help before it was too late. But the pleas went unheeded. He was lost in the maze of his own making, too far gone to find the way out.

In these last grotesque displays, Nicholas attained a tragic anti-apotheosis, embodying the horrors that result when humanity's base instincts reign unchecked. Here was ID untethered - no ethics, empathy or reason, just impulse and degradation. He had become both contemptible and pitiful - a cautionary effigy for an age gorging on extremes.

Yet even this serves as a form of martyrdom - Nicholas willingly transformed himself into the living embodiment of a cultural pathology. Like a sin eater consuming poison on society's behalf, he carries both villainy and pathos. We recoil, but his ruin implicates us all. For in gazing, we complete his sacrifice.

The Final Act

As another chaotic year drew to a close, Nicholas' predicament evoked both contempt and pathos. To critics, he was a clown who deserved ruin for degrading himself so shamelessly. But to supporters, he was a tortured soul crying out for help.

In truth, he was both. Nicholas chose his path, driven by compulsions he seemed unable to resist. But his story held tragedy - gifted talents and sensitivity corrupted in the crucible of viral fame. In the end, he became both villain and victim.

The year brought fleeting hopes of redemption between relapses into spectacle and self-destruction. For every glimmer of humanity, mania and darkness returned, stronger than before. The light flickered but could not hold.

Perhaps the cycle will continue indefinitely, or some epiphany may finally pierce Nicholas' delusions. But such outcomes are beyond prediction. His life remains hostage to demons beyond his current power to overcome. Only time and courage can exorcise them.

Yet whatever comes, Nicholas secured his strange legacy. He inhabited the extremes of an era like few others, revealing uncomfortable insights. His was the postmodern passion play - debasement not as means to an end, but the end itself. A purpose forged in meaninglessness.

In his fervor for attention, Nicholas sacrificed his dignity to become an antithesis to virtue. But we witnessed his fall with voyeuristic eyes, implicated in his corruption. For in the end, the jester only fulfills the role we prescribe.

So perhaps no neat moral emerges, only uncomfortable questions that outlive the spectacle. And in grappling with these, there is hope. For in the reckoning lies the path to wisdom. Where we choose to look determines what we see. The rest unfolds as it will - the final act remains unfinished.

www.ingramcontent.com/pod-product-compliance
Lightning Source LLC
LaVergne TN
LVHW051711050326
832903LV00032B/4135

*9 7 9 8 8 7 6 4 3 0 5 6 4 *